THE MANY MASKS OF

FALSE PREACHERS !

DON JOHNSON

THE MANY MASKS OF FALSE PREACHERS EXPOSED !

Ephesians 5:11 (NIV)
Have nothing to do with the fruitless deeds of darkness, but rather expose them.
2 Corinthians 11:14 (NIV)
And no wonder, for Satan himself masquerades as an angel of light.
Proverbs 26:24-26 (NIV)
[24] Enemies disguise themselves with their lips,
but in their hearts they harbor deceit.
[25] Though their speech is charming, do not believe them,
for seven abominations fill their hearts.
[26] Their malice may be concealed by deception,
but their wickedness will be exposed in the assembly.
1 Peter 5:8 (KJV)
Be sober, be vigilant; because your adversary the devil, as a roaring lion, walketh about, seeking whom he may devour:

THIS BOOK IS AN EXPOSE' OF THE THOUSANDS OF FALSE PREACHERS AND TEACHERS AND THEIR CHURCHES, NOT BY NAME, BUT BY THEIR DIRTY DEEDS! BY EXPOSING THE ROTTEN FRUIT THEY PRODUCE! BY EXOSING THE FALSE DOCTRINE THEY CREATE THAT CREATES A DARKNESS IN THEIR CHURCHES THAT BLINDS THEIR CONGREGATIONS FROM SEEING OR HEARING THE GOSPEL TRUTH OF JESUS CHRIST WHICH IS THE ONLY WAY TO ETERNAL LIFE WITH HIM! BY EXPOSING HOW THEIR DECEPTION DESTROYS THE LIVES, FAITH, AND SALVATION OF THOUSANDS OF LOST SOULS AND SHEEP WHO HAVE "FLOCKED" TO THEIR CHURCHES TO "BE SAVED" FROM THE EVIL IN THE WORLD AROUND THEM, ONLY TO FIND IT AMONG THEM IN THEIR CHURCHES! FALSE PREACHERS ARE AN ABOMINATION TO THE LORD !

Proverbs 12:22 (KJV)
Lying lips are abomination to the Lord: but they that deal truly are his delight.
Ephesians 5:11 (ESV)
[11] Take no part in the unfruitful works of darkness,
but instead expose them.
2 Peter 2:1 (NIV)
But there were also false prophets among the people, just as there will be false teachers among you. They will secretly introduce destructive heresies, even denying the sovereign Lord who bought them—bringing swift destruction on themselves.

INTRODUCTION

This book is an exposé of the many masks and hidden agendas of the thousands of today's false pastors, preachers, teachers, clerics, ministers, chaplains, parsons, reverends, missionaries, or anyone else claiming to represent The One True Living God of The Bible, Jesus Christ, God Almighty and The Holy Spirit, only instead when the masks are unveiled, they are found to be representing satan through their evil deception! This book exposes the many false teachings and doctrine we find in our churches today, through The Gospel Truth of God's Holy Word! The pastor of your Church should be leading his congregation to Salvation through The Gospel Truth of God's Holy Word! Instead, we find many Churches today led by blind false preachers who use scripture out of context to create false doctrine that will lead their congregations away from the Gospel Truth of Christ and Salvation! This book will show you many examples of practices, policies, programs, and teachings that go against the teachings of the Gospel!

BLIND GUIDES, FALSE TEACHERS, AND PREACHERS, ARE LEADING OUR CHURCHES AND THEIR MEMBERS TO HELL WITH THEIR FALSE DOCTRINES !

2 Peter 2:1 (NIV)
But there were also false prophets among the people, just as there will be false teachers among you. They will secretly introduce destructive heresies, even denying the sovereign Lord who bought them—bringing swift destruction on themselves.

JESUS SAID ...

"BEWARE"

"OF FALSE PROPHETS, WHICH COME TO YOU IN SHEEP'S CLOTHING, BUT INWARDLY THEY ARE RAVENING WOLVES."
Matthew 7:15 (KJV)

YOUR FALSE PREACHER SAYS

"TRUST ME,"

AND I'LL LEAD YOU TO HEAVEN, AND MAKE YOU HEALTHY AND WEALTHY!

WHO ARE YOU GOING TO BELIEVE?

SATAN

HAS ALWAYS BEEN THE CHRISTIANS #1 ENEMY! WELL CAMOUFLAGED BEHIND THE PULPIT IN A MASK AS YOUR FRIENDLY NEIGHBORHOOD PASTOR! USING GOD'S WORD OUT OF CONTEXT TO MAKE YOU BELIEVE HIS MANY LIES THAT WILL LEAD YOU AWAY FROM

CHRIST!

Matthew 4:10
[10] Jesus said to him, "Away from me, Satan! For it is written: 'Worship the Lord your God, and serve him only.'

FALSE TEACHERS AND PREACHERS WEAR MANY LAYERS OF MASKS TO DECEIVE EVEN THE MOST VIGILANT, OBSERVANT WATCHMAN IN THE CONGREGATION ! THEIR DECEPTION HAS BEEN CRAFTED BY THE DEVIL !

Proverbs 26:26 (NIV)
26 Their malice may be concealed by deception,
but their wickedness will be exposed in the assembly.
Jeremiah 9:6 (NIV)
6 You live in the midst of deception;
in their deceit they refuse to acknowledge me,"
declares the Lord.

9

BEWARE ...

FALSE TEACHERS AND PREACHERS ARE LIKE CHAMELEONS, CAPABLE OF CHANGING THEIR MANY MASKS AND FALSE IDENTITIES IN THE BLINK OF AN EYE!

Titus 1:10

10 For there are many rebellious people who engage in useless talk and deceive others. This is especially true of those who insist on circumcision for salvation.

2 Corinthians 11:14 (NIV)
And no wonder, for Satan himself masquerades as an angel of light.

BEWARE ...

FALSE TEACHERS AND PREACHERS USE THE SCRIPTURE IN GOD'S WORD OUT OF CONTEXT TO DECIEVE THEIR FLOCK AND LEAD THEM ASTRAY !

2 Peter 2:1 (NIV)
But there were also false prophets among the people, just as there will be false teachers among you. They will secretly introduce destructive heresies, even denying the sovereign Lord who bought them—bringing swift destruction on themselves.

BEWARE !
MANY BLIND
LEADERS AND
FALSE PREACHERS

DECEIVE THEIR FLOCK BY
USING SCRIPTURE OUT OF
CONTEXT TO CREATE FALSE
DOCTINE THAT BLINDS ITS
RECIPIENTS !

Jeremiah 9:6 (NIV)
⁶ You live in the midst of deception;
in their deceit they refuse to acknowledge me,"
declares the LORD.
Galatians 6:7 (NIV)
⁷ Do not be deceived: God cannot be mocked.
A man reaps what he sows.

BEWARE OF BLIND LEADERS AND FALSE PREACHERS WHO ARE FILLED WITH PRIDE, ARROGANCE, AND SELF-RIGHTEOUSNESS, IN THE PULPIT! INSTEAD OF LOVE, HUMILITY, AND TRUTH!

Matthew 23:24-25
[24] *You blind guides! You strain out a gnat but swallow a camel.*
[25] *"Woe to you, teachers of the law and Pharisees, you hypocrites! You clean the outside of the cup and dish, but inside they are full of greed and self-indulgence.*
Matthew 15:14 (ESV)
14 Let them alone; they are blind guides. And if the blind lead the blind, both will fall into a pit."

BEWARE OF

BLIND LEADERS AND FALSE PREACHERS WHO USE SCRIPTURE OUT OF CONTEXT TO SQUEEZE THE LAST DOLLAR OUT OF YOUR WALLET!

Isaiah 56:10
10 For the leaders of my people— the Lord's watchmen, his shepherds— are blind and ignorant. They are like silent watchdogs that give no warning when danger comes. They love to lie around, sleeping and dreaming.
Matthew 23:15-17
15 "What sorrow awaits you teachers of religious law and you Pharisees. Hypocrites! For you cross land and sea to make one convert, and then you turn that person into twice the child of hell, you yourselves are!
16 "Blind guides! What sorrow awaits you! For you say that it means nothing to swear 'by God's Temple,' but that it is binding to swear 'by the gold in the Temple.' 17 Blind fools! Which is more important—the gold or the Temple that makes the gold sacred?

BEWARE OF

BLIND LEADERS AND FALSE PREACHERS WHO USE SCRIPTURE OUT OF CONTEXT TO CONVINCE YOU THAT YOU ARE STILL UNDER THE LAW OF THE OLD TESTAMENT !

Matthew 23:24-25

24 You blind guides! You strain out a gnat but swallow a camel.
25 "Woe to you, teachers of the law and Pharisees, you hypocrites! You clean the outside of the cup and dish, but inside they are full of greed and self-indulgence.

Isaiah 56:10

10 For the leaders of my people— the Lord's watchmen, his shepherds— are blind and ignorant. They are like silent watchdogs that give no warning when danger comes. They love to lie around, sleeping and dreaming.

BEWARE OF

BLIND LEADERS AND FALSE PREACHERS WHO USE SCRIPTURE OUT OF CONTEXT TO CONDEMN SINNERS INTO BELIEVING IT IS WORKS NOT GRACE THAT SAVES US !

Ephesians 2:8-9
8 For it is by grace you have been saved, through faith—and this is not from yourselves, it is the gift of God— 9 not by works, so that no one can boast.
2 Peter 2:1 (NIV)
But there were also false prophets among the people, just as there will be false teachers among you. They will secretly introduce destructive heresies, even denying the sovereign Lord who bought them—bringing swift destruction on themselves.

BEWARE OF

BLIND LEADERS AND FALSE PREACHERS WHO USE SCRIPTURE OUT OF CONTEXT TO CONDEMN SINNERS INTO BELIEVING THEY CAN BUY THEIR WAY INTO HEAVEN !

Ephesians 1:7
7 In him we have redemption through his blood, the forgiveness of sins, in accordance with the riches of God's grace
Acts 8:20
20 Peter answered: "May your money perish with you, because you thought you could buy the gift of God with money!

THE MANY MASKS OF FALSE PREACHERS

BEWARE OF

BLIND LEADERS AND FALSE PREACHERS WHO USE SCRIPTURE OUT OF CONTEXT TO CONDEMN SINNERS INTO BELIEVING THE FORGIVENESS OF THEIR SIN CAN BE BOUGHT !

Acts 8:20
20 Peter answered: "May your money perish with you, because you thought you could buy the gift of God with money!
Colossians 1:13-14
13 For he has rescued us from the dominion of darkness and brought us into the kingdom of the Son he loves, 14 in whom we have redemption, the forgiveness of sins.

BEWARE OF BLIND LEADERS AND FALSE PREACHERS

WHO ARE PROFESSIONALLY EDUCATED IN THE ART OF DECEPTION ! BUT ARE COMPLETELY IGNORANT OF THE GOSPEL TRUTH OF JESUS CHRIST !

Jeremiah 9:6 (NIV)
6 You live in the midst of deception; in their deceit they refuse to acknowledge me," declares the LORD.

BEWARE OF BLIND LEADERS AND FALSE PREACHERS

WHO TAKE CLASSES ON INCREASING CHURCH ATTENDENCE OUT OF PERSONAL GREED, RATHER THAN OTHERS SALVATION !

Mark 8:36 (NIV)
What good is it for someone to gain the whole world, yet forfeit their soul? Jude 11 (NLT)

11 What sorrow awaits them! For they follow in the footsteps of Cain, who killed his brother. Like Balaam, they deceive people for money. And like Korah, they perish in their rebellion.

BEWARE OF BLIND LEADERS AND FALSE PREACHERS

WHO TOLERATE SINFUL BEHAVIOR IN THEIR CHURCHES IN RETURN FOR GENEROUS TITHES !

1 Timothy 6:10 (NIV)
For the love of money is a root of all kinds of evil. Some people, eager for money, have wandered from the faith and pierced themselves with many griefs.
Ephesians 4:19 (NIV)
19 Having lost all sensitivity, they have given themselves over to sensuality so as to indulge in every kind of impurity, and they are full of greed.
Jude 11 (NLT)11 What sorrow awaits them! For they follow in the footsteps of Cain, who killed his brother. Like Balaam, they deceive people for money. And like Korah, they perish in their rebellion.

DO NOT BE DECEIVED BY BLIND LEADERS AND FALSE PREACHERS

WHO USE SCRIPTURE OUT OF CONTEXT TO WIN SOULS TO CHRIST !

Matthew 23:15
15 "What sorrow awaits you teachers of religious law and you Pharisees. Hypocrites! For you cross land and sea to make one convert, and then you turn that person into twice the child of hell you yourselves are!
Acts 15:5
5 Then some of the believers who belonged to the party of the Pharisees stood up and said, "The Gentiles must be circumcised and required to keep the law of Moses."

DO NOT BE DECEIVED BY BLIND LEADERS AND FALSE PREACHERS

WHO BLASPHEMY GOD THROUGH THE TEACHING OF FALSE DOCTRINE !

2 Timothy 4:3 (NIV)
3 For the time will come when people will not put up with sound doctrine. Instead, to suit their own desires, they will gather around them a great number of teachers to say what their itching ears want to hear.

Hebrews 13:9 (NIV)
9 Do not be carried away by all kinds of strange teachings. It is good for our hearts to be strengthened by grace, not by eating ceremonial foods, which is of no benefit to those who do so.

BEWARE OF BLIND LEADERS AND FALSE PREACHERS WHO CREATE THEIR OWN FALSE DOCTRINE TO CREATE AND PLEASE THEIR OWN PERSONAL FOLLOWERS ! RATHER THAN FOLLOWERS OF CHRIST !

2 Timothy 4:3 (NIV)
3 For the time will come when people will not put up with sound doctrine. Instead, to suit their own desires, they will gather around them a great number of teachers to say what their itching ears want to hear.
Matthew 4:19 (NIV)
"Come, follow me," Jesus said, "and I will send you out to fish for people."

BEWARE OF BLIND LEADERS AND FALSE PREACHERS WHO CREATE THEIR OWN PERVERTED AND DILUTED FALSE GOSPEL TO APPEASE AND DECEIVE THEIR AUDIENCE AND DISILLUSIONED FOLLOWERS !

Galatians 1:5-7 (ESV)
No Other Gospel
[5]*to whom be the glory forever and ever. Amen.*
[6]*I am astonished that you are so quickly deserting him who called you in the grace of Christ and are turning to a different gospel—* [7]*not that there is another one, but there are some who trouble you and want to distort the gospel of Christ.*

A GODLY PASTOR

WANTS YOU TO BE AS THE BEREANS IN ACTS 17:11 AND SEARCH THE SCRIPTURE DAILY TO SEE IF WHAT HE TEACHES WILL HOLD UP TO THE GOSPEL TRUTH OF

JESUS CHRIST !

Acts 17:11 (NIV)
[11] Now the Berean Jews were of more noble character than those in Thessalonica, for they received the message with great eagerness and examined the Scriptures every day to see if what Paul said was true.

Proverbs 30:8 (NIV)
[8] Keep falsehood and lies far from me; give me neither poverty nor riches, but give me only my daily bread.

BEWARE OF BLIND LEADERS AND FALSE PREACHERS WHO PREACH THE PROSPERITY GOSPEL AND TELL YOU THE MORE MONEY YOU GIVE TO THEM, THE MORE MONEY GOD WILL GIVE BACK TO YOU !

Matthew 23:16-17 (NIV)
16 "Woe to you, blind guides! You say, 'If anyone swears by the temple, it means nothing; but anyone who swears by the gold of the temple is bound by that oath.' 17 You blind fools! Which is greater: the gold, or the temple that makes the gold sacred?
Matthew 21:13 (KJV)
13 And said unto them, It is written, My house shall be called the house of prayer; but ye have made it a den of thieves.

BEWARE !
MANY
BLIND LEADERS AND
FALSE PREACHERS
DECEIVE THEIR FLOCK BY USING SCRIPTURE OUT OF CONTEXT TO CREATE FALSE DOCTINE THAT BLINDS ITS RECIPIENTS !

Jeremiah 9:6 (NIV)
6 You live in the midst of deception;
in their deceit they refuse to acknowledge me,"
declares the LORD.
Galatians 6:7 (NIV)
7 Do not be deceived: God cannot be mocked.
A man reaps what he sows.

BEWARE !

DO NOT BE DECEIVED BY BLIND LEADERS AND FALSE PREACHERS WHO WOULD RATHER BUILD MEGA CHURCHES AND BANK ACCOUNTS RATHER THAN SAVE LOST SOULS !

Luke 21:8 (NIV)
[8] He replied: "Watch out that you are not deceived. For many will come in my name, claiming, 'I am he,' and, 'The time is near.' Do not follow them.
2 Corinthians 11:3 (NIV)
3 But I am afraid that just as Eve was deceived by the serpent's cunning, your minds may somehow be led astray from your sincere and pure devotion to Christ.

BEWARE !

MANY
BLIND LEADERS AND FALSE PREACHERS REFUSE TO SERVE CHRIST THROUGH EVANGELISTIC MISSIONARY PROGRAMS FOR OUR JAILS, PRISONS, AND HOMELESS SHELTERS !

Mark 10:45 (NIV)
45 For even the Son of Man did not come to be served, but to serve, and to give his life as a ransom for many."
Romans 16:17-18 (NIV)17
I urge you, brothers and sisters, to watch out for those who cause divisions and put obstacles in your way that are contrary to the teaching you have learned. Keep away from them. 18 For such people are not serving our Lord Christ, but their own appetites. By smooth talk and flattery they deceive the minds of naive people.

BEWARE OF FALSE CHURCHES

LED BY BLIND LEADERS AND FALSE PREACHERS WHO DISTORT THE GOSPEL OF JESUS CHRIST AND TWIST GOD'S TRUTH TO FIT THEIR OWN SELFISH MOTIVES !

Revelation 22:18-19 (NIV)

[18] I warn everyone who hears the words of the prophecy of this scroll: If anyone adds anything to them, God will add to that person the plagues described in this scroll. [19] And if anyone takes words away from this scroll of prophecy, God will take away from that person any share in the tree of life and in the Holy City, which are described in this scroll.

BEWARE !

IF YOUR CHURCH ISN'T BUSY SERVING THE LOST SOULS IN YOUR CHURCH AND COMMUNITY, AND LEADING THEM TO CHRIST, THEN YOUR LEADER IS A BLIND GUIDE !

Matthew 15:14 (NLT)
So, ignore them. They are blind guides leading the
blind, and if one blind person guides another, they
will both fall into a ditch." Ephesians 3:7 (NIV)
I became a servant of this gospel by the gift of
God's grace given me through the working of his
power.

BEWARE !
A GODLY CHURCH
NEEDS TO BE DEDICATED TO SHARING THE GOSPEL OF JESUS CHRIST WITH OTHERS AND LEADING THEM TO SALVATION ! NOT TO SUNDAY BRUNCHES, BANQUETS, BARBEQUES, AND FOOD DRIVES !

2 Corinthians 9:13 (NIV)

13 Because of the service by which you have proved yourselves, others will praise God for the obedience that accompanies your confession of the gospel of Christ, and for your generosity in sharing with them and with everyone else.

A GODLY PASTOR'S #1 PRIORITY SHOULD BE TO LEAD HIS ENTIRE FLOCK OF SHEEP TO A CLOSER, DEEPER, PERSONAL RELATIONSHIP WITH OUR SAVIOR, JESUS CHRIST, AND DO SO THROUGH THE TRUTH OF HIS GOSPEL ! BEWARE OF THOSE WHO DON'T !

Ephesians 4:10-12 (NIV)
[10] He who descended is the very one who ascended higher than all the heavens, in order to fill the whole universe.) [11] So Christ himself gave the apostles, the prophets, the evangelists, the pastors and teachers,[12] to equip his people for works of service, so that the body of Christ may be built up

BEWARE OF

ATTENDING A CHURCH

LED BY FALSE TEACHERS AND PREACHERS WHO SAY TITHING, READING THE BIBLE, PRAYING AND READING DEVOTIONALS, WILL GET YOU INTO HEAVEN! ONLY REPENTANCE AND A GENUINE, CLOSE PERSONAL RELATIONSIP WITH JESUS CHRIST GUARANTIES SALVATION !

Acts 4:12 (KJV)
Neither is there salvation in any other: for there is none other name under heaven given among men, whereby we must be saved.

BEWARE OF FALSE TEACHERS AND PREACHERS WHO PREACH THE OLD TESTAMENT LAW WITHOUT RECOGNIZING OR ACKNOWLEDGING THE GRACE OF THE GOSPEL OF JESUS CHRIST THAT REPLACED IT !

Matthew 26:28 (KJV)
28 For this is my blood of the new testament, which is shed for many for the remission of sins.

Ephesians 2:8-9 (KJV)
8 For by grace are ye saved through faith; and that not of yourselves: it is the gift of God: 9 Not of works, lest any man should boast.

A GODLY PASTOR AND CHURCH

WILL DEVOTE MOST OF ITS RESOURCES, TIME, AND ENERGY, TO EVANGELISM AND THE MISSIONS FIELD FROM ITS OWN NEIGHBORHOOD, TO THE ENDS OF THE EARTH !
INSTEAD OUR FALSE PREACHERS ARE DEVOTED TO SERVING THE DEVILS PROSPERITY GOSPEL !

Ecclesiastes 5:10 (NIV)
[10] Whoever loves money never has enough; whoever loves wealth is never satisfied with their income. This too is meaningless.

WORSHIPPING YOUR FALSE PREACHER

WILL LEAD YOU TO HELL, <u>NOT</u> HEAVEN ! AND THE WORST OF THE WORST FALSE PREACHERS STRUT THEIR STUFF ON THE STAGE SEEKING YOUR ADORATION LIKE CLOWNS IN A THREE RING CIRCUS !

Matthew 4:10 (NIV)
10 Jesus said to him, "Away from me, Satan! For it is written: 'Worship the Lord your God, and serve him only.'
Matthew 15:9 (NIV)
9 They worship me in vain; their teachings are merely human rules.'

BEWARE !

ATTENDING A CHURCH LED BY A FALSE PREACHER AND BLIND GUIDE WILL LEAD YOU TO SATAN, <u>NOT</u> TO JESUS CHRIST! FALSE TEACHERS AND PREACHERS HAVE DRIFTED AWAY FROM GOD'S TRUTH AND THE GOSPEL OF JESUS CHRIST, AND ARE FOLLOWING THE DEVIL !

Ecclesiastes 5:1 (ESV)
Guard your steps when you go to the house of God. To draw near to listen is better than to offer the sacrifice of fools, for they do not know that they are doing evil.

BEWARE !

THERE ARE MANY FALSE GODS AND ANTI-CHRISTS ALL AROUND US ! CREATED BY SATAN WHO HAS LED FALSE TEACHERS AND PREACHERS TO LEAD US ASTRAY BY CREATING FALSE DOCTRINE !

1 John 2:18 (NIV)
[18] Dear children, this is the last hour; and as you have heard that the antichrist is coming, even now many antichrists have come. This is how we know it is the last hour.

2 John 7 New International Version (NIV)
7 I say this because many deceivers, who do not acknowledge Jesus Christ as coming in the flesh, have gone out into the world. Any such person is the deceiver and the antichrist.

BEWARE OF ATTENDING CHURCHES

THAT ARE LED BY FALSE PREACHERS AND BLIND GUIDES WHO SUBSCRIBE TO SECULAR TEACHINGS, PROGRAMS AND PRACTICES OF THIS WORLD, THAT WILL LEAD YOU DEEPER INTO THE WORLD OF SATAN AND AWAY FROM CHRIST !

2 Corinthians 11:3 (NIV) But I am afraid that just as Eve was deceived by the serpent's cunning, your minds may somehow be led astray from your sincere and pure devotion to Christ.

BEWARE OF BLIND LEADERS AND FALSE PREACHERS

WHO PREACH ANYTHING THAT IS NOT FROM THE WORD OF GOD ! IF IT IS NOT FROM THE WORD OF GOD, IT IS FROM THE DEVIL !

1 Peter 5:8 (KJV)
Be sober, be vigilant; because your adversary the devil, as a roaring lion, walketh about, seeking whom he may devour:
1 John 4:3 (KJV)
And every spirit that confesseth not that Jesus Christ is come in the flesh is not of God: and this is that spirit of antichrist, whereof ye have heard that it should come; and even now already is it in the world.

IF YOUR PASTOR ISN'T PREACHING "REPENTANCE," HE ISN'T A PASTOR, BUT A FALSE PREACHER LED BY SATAN, NOT THE HOLY SPIRIT! REPENTANCE IS THE ONLY WAY TO SALVATION !

Acts 2:38 (KJV)
[38] Then Peter said unto them, Repent, and be baptized every one of you in the name of Jesus Christ for the remission of sins, and ye shall receive the gift of the Holy Ghost.

Acts 26:20 (NIV)
20 First to those in Damascus, then to those in Jerusalem and in all Judea, and then to the Gentiles, I preached that they should repent and turn to God and demonstrate their repentance by their deeds.

BEHIND THE MANY MASKS OF FALSE PREACHERS,

WE SEE HYPOCRICY, PRIDE, ARROGANCE, ANGER, GREED, AND IGNORANCE ! THESE ARE SOME OF THE MANY SIGNS OF SOME ONE FOLLOWING SATAN, "NOT" JESUS CHRIST !

Proverbs 21:24 (ASV)
24 The proud and haughty man, scoffer is his name; He worketh in the arrogance of pride. Proverbs 8:13 (NLT) 13 All who fear the Lord will hate evil. Therefore, I hate pride and arrogance, corruption and perverse speech. 2 Timothy 3:4 (NLT) 4 They will betray their friends, be reckless, be puffed up with pride, and love pleasure rather than God.

FALSE PREACHERS

ARE THOSE WHO SPEND THEIR TIME PREPARING THEIR SERMONS AND MESSAGES FROM THE GOLF COURSE, OR A PRIVATE ISLAND IN THE BAHAMAS, RATHER THAN FROM THE GOSPEL !

Matthew 24:14 (KJV)
14 And this gospel of the kingdom shall be preached in all the world for a witness unto all nations; and then shall the end come.
2 Peter 2:1 King James Version (KJV)
2 But there were false prophets also among the people, even as there shall be false teachers among you, who privily shall bring in damnable heresies, even denying the Lord that bought them, and bring upon themselves swift destruction.

FALSE PASTORS AND PREACHERS ARE SINNERS ALSO, JUST LIKE THE REST OF US ! BUT WHEN THEY DON'T ADMIT IT, THEY'VE NOT REPENTED AND ARE NOT SAVED AND UNWORTHY OF THE PULPIT AND BECOME FALSE PREACHERS !

1 Corinthians 11:27 (KJV)
27 Wherefore whosoever shall eat this bread, and drink this cup of the Lord, unworthily, shall be guilty of the body and blood of the Lord.
Ephesians 4:1 (NIV)
4 As a prisoner for the Lord, then, I urge you to live a life worthy of the calling you have received.

YOUR CHURCHES
FOOD BANK OR HOMELESS PROGRAMS NEED TO BE SERVING BIGGER HELPINGS OF "THE BREAD OF LIFE", RATHER THAN MEAT AND POTATOES AND WORLDLY ENTERTAINMENT!

John 6:51 (KJV)
51 I am the living bread which came down from heaven: if any man eat of this bread, he shall live for ever: and the bread that I will give is my flesh, which I will give for the life of the world.
John 6:35 (KJV)
35 And Jesus said unto them, I am the bread of life: he that cometh to me shall never hunger; and he that believeth on me shall never thirst.

DON'T BLAME JESUS !

BLAME YOUR FALSE TEACHER AND PREACHER FOR YOUR DISILLUSIONMENT OF THE CHURCH AND THE WORLD WHERE IT EXISTS ! ONLY THE TEACHINGS OF THE GOSPEL TRUTH OF JESUS CHRIST WILL BRING YOU THE PEACE, JOY, AND LIGHT OF SALVATION !

Galatians 1:9 King James Version (KJV)
[9] As we said before, so say I now again, if any man preach any other gospel unto you than that ye have received, let him be accursed.

THE REASON

THERE IS SO MUCH DECEPTION IN THE WORLD TODAY, IS BECAUSE THERE IS SO MUCH DECEPTION IN THE CHURCH TODAY BY OUR FALSE TEACHERS AND PREACHERS !

Jeremiah 9:6 (NIV)
⁶ You live in the midst of deception;
in their deceit they refuse to acknowledge me,"
declares the LORD.

Titus 1:10 (NIV)
10 For there are many rebellious people, full of
meaningless talk and deception, especially those of
the circumcision group.

Proverbs 26:26 (NIV)
26 Their malice may be concealed by deception,
but their wickedness will be exposed in the
assembly.

CHRIST CAME TO SET US FREE !

FALSE PREACHERS AND BLIND GUIDES ARE HERE TO KEEP US AWAY FROM THE GOSPEL TRUTH OF JESUS CHRIST, AND KEEP US IN THE BONDAGE OF THE SINFUL WORLD, AND UNDER THE INFLUENCE OF THE DEVILS LIES !

John 8:31-33 (NIV)

To the Jews who had believed him, Jesus said, "If you hold to my teaching, you are really my disciples. [32] Then you will know the truth, and the truth will set you free." [33] They answered him, We be Abraham's seed, and were never in bondage to any man: how sayest thou, Ye shall be made free?

MANY FALSE PREACHERS TODAY

TRY TO RECRUIT NEW CONVERTS INTO THEIR PRIVATE CULTS WITH BARBEQUES, BRUNCHES, AND BANQUETS, RATHER THAN FEEDING THEM WITH THE GOSPEL TRUTH OF JESUS CHRIST!

John 6:51 (KJV)

51 I am the living bread which came down from heaven: if any man eat of this bread, he shall live forever: and the bread that I will give is my flesh, which I will give for the life of the world.

John 6:35 (KJV)

35 And Jesus said unto them, I am the bread of life: he that cometh to me shall never hunger; and he that believeth on me shall never thirst.

BEWARE !
CHRISTIAN
BROTHERS AND
SISTERS !

YOUR COMFORTABLE LITTLE NEIGHBORHOOD CHURCH MAY BE LITTLE MORE THAN THE PRIVATE CULT OF A DEMENTED FALSE PREACHER ! READ THE SCRIPTURE DAILY TO ENSURE YOU'RE HEARING THE GOSPEL TRUTH !

Acts 17:11 (NIV)

[11] Now the Berean Jews were of more noble character than those in Thessalonica, for they received the message with great eagerness and examined the Scriptures every day to see if what Paul said was true.

FALSE PREACHERS
ARE LIKE DRUNKARDS, IN DENIAL OF THEIR SINFUL BEHAVIOR ! REFUSING TO TAKE HEED FROM ANYONE WHO TRIES TO REBUKE THEM !

Proverbs 1:23-25 (NIV)
23 Repent at my rebuke! Then I will pour out my thoughts to you,
I will make known to you my teachings 24 But since you refuse to listen when I call and no one pays attention when I stretch out my hand, 25 since you disregard all my advice
and do not accept my rebuke,
Proverbs 26:9 (NIV)
⁹ Like a thornbush in a drunkard's hand
is a proverb in the mouth of a fool.
1 Timothy 5:20 (NIV)
20 But those elders who are sinning you are to reprove before everyone, so that the others may take warning.

FALSE PREACHERS

WITH SWOLEN HEADS, FAT BANK ACCOUNTS, AND A LOVE FOR WORLDLY PLEASURES, ARE DANGEROUS, RAVENOUS WOLVES IN SHEEP'S CLOTHING, SEEKING TO LEAD YOU ASTRAY !

Matthew 7:15 (NASB)

[15] **"Beware of the false prophets, who come to you in sheep's clothing, but inwardly are ravenous wolves.**

Galatians 6: (KJV)

3 For if a man think himself to be something, when he is nothing, he deceiveth himself.

1 John 2:16 (KJV)

16 For all that is in the world, the lust of the flesh, and the lust of the eyes, and the pride of life, is not of the Father, but is of the world.

MANY FALSE TEACHERS AND PREACHERS

USE THEIR POSITION OF AUTHORITY TO TAKE ADVANTAGE OF FEMALE CHURCH MEMBERS IN VULNERABLE SITUATIONS! ESPECIALLY IN COUNSELING

1 Timothy 3:2 English Standard Version (ESV)
2 Therefore an overseer must be above reproach, the husband of one wife] sober-minded, self-controlled, respectable, hospitable, able to teach,

1 Peter 5:8 King James Version (KJV)
8 Be sober, be vigilant; because your adversary the devil, as a roaring lion, walketh about, seeking whom he may devour:

CHRISTIANS BEWARE ! ....

ARE YOU BEING TAUGHT THE GOSPEL TRUTH OF JESUS CHRIST, OR FALSE DOCTRINE THROUGH THE MISINTERPRETATION AND TWISTING OF SCRIPTURE BY A FALSE PREACHER ?

Proverbs 14:8 (NIV)
8 The wisdom of the prudent is to give thought to their ways,
but the folly of fools is deception.
Proverbs 26:26 (NIV)
Their malice may be concealed by deception,
but their wickedness will be exposed in the assembly.

IF YOUR PASTOR

IS STILL DRAGGING ONE FOOT IN THE DARK, EVIL WORLD OF SATAN, HE HAS NOT SURRENDERED HIS LIFE TO JESUS CHRIST, NOR IS HE LIVING ACCORDING TO THE GOSPEL OF JESUS CHRIST ! HE IS A FALSE TEACHER WHO NEEDS TO LET GO OF THE WORLD !

Psalm 31:6 (NIV)
6 I hate those who cling to worthless idols;
as for me, I trust in the LORD. Romans 12:9
(NIV) Love must be sincere. Hate what is evil; cling
to what is good. 1 John 2:15 (KJV)
Love not the world, neither the things that are in
the world. If any man love the world, the love of the
Father is not in him.

THE NARROW ROAD
IS A ONE WAY PATH WITHOUT EXITS AND TRAVELED BY BORN AGAIN CHRISTIANS SEEKING TO FOLLOW THE GOSPEL TRUTH OF JESUS CHRIST TO THE NARROW GATE INTO ETERNAL LIFE ! YOU WILL NOT FIND ANY FALSE TEACHERS AND PREACHERS ON THAT PATH WITH YOU !

Matthew 7:13-14 (NIV)
The Narrow and Wide Gates
[13] *"Enter through the narrow gate. For wide is the gate and broad is the road that leads to destruction, and many enter through it.* [14] *But small is the gate and narrow the road that leads to life, and only a few find it.*

FALSE TEACHERS AND PREACHERS TRAVEL THE WIDE ROAD TO DEATH AND DESTRUCTION BY DECEIVING GODS LOST SHEEP WHO FOLLOW THEM ! THEY PREACH FALSE DOCTRINE, HERESY, AND BLASPHEMY THAT CONTRADICT THE HOLY WORD OF GOD !

Matthew 7:13-14 (NIV)
The Narrow and Wide Gates
[13] *"Enter through the narrow gate. For wide is the gate and broad is the road that leads to destruction, and many enter through it.* [14] *But small is the gate and narrow the road that leads to life, and only a few find it.*

FALSE TEACHERS AND PREACHERS

HAVE DECEIVED THEMSELVES IN THEIR OWN IGNORANCE AND BLINDNESS, BELIEVING THAT GOD CAN'T SEE THEIR EVIL DEEDS ! GOD CLEARLY SEES THEIR EVIL WAYS AND WILL REWARD THEM JUSTLY ACCORDING TO THE SCRIPTURE !

Proverbs 24:20 (KJV)
[20] **For there shall be no reward to the evil man; the candle of the wicked shall be put out.**

A FALSE PREACHER CANNOT TEACH THE GOSPEL OF JESUS CHRIST USING WORLDLY TACTICS, PROGRAMS, PRACTICES, AND ENTERTAINMENT, THEY DON'T MIX ANYMORE THAN OIL AND WATER DON'T MIX ! NEITHER CAN A LOST SOUL BE SAVED THROUGH WORLDLY DEEDS !

1 John 2:15 (KJV)
15 Love not the world, neither the things that are in the world. If any man love the world, the love of the Father is not in him.

MANY FALSE PREACHERS

TEACH SALVATION THROUGH GOOD WORKS ! THAT IS A LIE STRAIGHT FROM THE DEVIL'S LIPS ! SALVATION COMES ONLY BY GRACE ALONE, THROUGH FAITH ALONE, IN THE NAME OF CHRIST ALONE !

John 3:16 King James Version (KJV)
16 For God so loved the world, that he gave his only begotten Son, that whosoever believeth in him should not perish, but have everlasting life.
Ephesians 2:8-9 (KJV)
8 For by grace are ye saved through faith; and that not of yourselves: it is the gift of God: 9 Not of works, lest any man should boast.

FALSE PREACHERS

LIVE IN MANSIONS, FLY IN LEAR JETS, DRIVE EXOTIC, EXPENSIVE CARS, DINE IN ELEGANT RESTAURANTS, ETC., WHILE JESUS LIVED IN TENTS, RODE ON DONKEYS, AND ATE FISH HE CAUGHT IN NETS!

Matthew 24:24 (ASV)[24] *For there shall arise false Christs, and false prophets, and shall show great signs and wonders; so as to lead astray, if possible, even the elect. 2 Peter 2:1 (KJV)*
But there were false prophets also among the people, even as there shall be false teachers among you, who privily shall bring in damnable heresies, even denying the Lord that bought them, and bring upon themselves swift destruction.

TRYING TO REBUKE A FALSE PREACHER

IS LIKE REBUKING A DRUNKARD, OR THE WIND ! AN EFFORT IN FUTILITY ! UNLESS IT IS GOD'S WILL FOR THERE TO BE A CHANGE !

Romans 9:15-16 (KJV)
[15] For he saith to Moses, I will have mercy on whom I will have mercy, and I will have compassion on whom I will have compassion. [16] So then it is not of him that willeth, nor of him that runneth, but of God that sheweth mercy.
Matthew 8:26 (KJV)
26 And he saith unto them, Why are ye fearful, O ye of little faith? Then he arose, and rebuked the winds and the sea; and there was a great calm.
Proverbs 24:25 (KJV)
25 But to them that rebuke him shall be delight, and a good blessing shall come upon them.

IF YOUR CHURCH'S #1 PRIORITY ISN'T EVANGELISM AND SALVATION, THEN YOUR PASTOR IS A FALSE PREACHER AND A BLIND GUIDE! IGNORING THE GOSPELS GREAT COMMISSION !

Matthew 28:19-20 (KJV)

[19] Go ye therefore, and teach all nations, baptizing them in the name of the Father, and of the Son, and of the Holy Ghost:

[20] Teaching them to observe all things whatsoever I have commanded you: and, lo, I am with you always, even unto the end of the world. Amen.

IF YOUR CHURCH ISN'T TEACHING THAT SALVATION REQUIRES REPENTANCE, THEN YOUR PASTOR IS A FALSE PREACHER AND BLIND GUIDE ! IGNORING THE GOSPELS SIMPLE TRUTH !

Acts 2:38 (KJV)
38 Then Peter said unto them, Repent, and be baptized every one of you in the name of Jesus Christ for the remission of sins, and ye shall receive the gift of the Holy Ghost. Matthew 3:8 (KJV)
8 Bring forth therefore fruits meet for repentance:

A GODLY PASTOR,

WILL FOLLOW CHRIST AND SERVE LIKE JOHN THE BAPTIST, SEARCHING IN THE WILDERNESS AND DARK CORNERS OF THE WORLD, TO FIND AND CONVERT AND BAPTIZE LOST SOULS INTO THE KINGDOM OF GOD !

Mark 1:4-5 (NIV)
[4] And so John the Baptist appeared in the wilderness, preaching a baptism of repentance for the forgiveness of sins. [5] The whole Judean countryside and all the people of Jerusalem went out to him. Confessing their sins, they were baptized by him in the Jordan River.

FALSE TEACHERS AND PREACHERS

WILL PREACH FALSE DOCTRINE, LIES, HERESY, AND BLASPHEMY FOR ONE HOUR A WEEK, BEG YOU FOR YOUR LAST DOLLAR, THEN TAKE THE NEXT SIX DAYS OFF TO PLAY GOLF,

Acts 20:29 (KJV)
29 For I know this, that after my departing shall grievous wolves enter in among you, not sparing the flock.
Matthew 10:15-16 (KJV)
15 Verily I say unto you, It shall be more tolerable for the land of Sodom and Gomorrha in the day of judgment, than for that city.
16 Behold, I send you forth as sheep in the midst of wolves: be ye therefore wise as serpents, and harmless as doves.

GODLY PASTORS

WHO FOLLOW CHRIST WILL SPEND SIX DAYS A WEEK FISHING FOR LOST SOULS AND SHEEP IN ALL THE DARK PLACES TO THE ENDS OF THE EARTH ! AND WILL ENCOURAGE HIS CONGREGATION TO DO THE SAME ! WE ARE ALL CALLED TO BE FISHERS OF MEN !

Matthew 4:19 (KJV)
And he saith unto them, Follow me,
and I will make you fishers of men.

FALSE TEACHERS AND PREACHERS BY DEFINITION ARE CULT LEADERS, LEADING LOST SOULS TO DEATH AND DESTRUCTION INSTEAD OF TO SALVATION AND ETERNAL LIFE WITH CHRIST!

Definition of cult; *noun* ; a system of religious veneration and devotion directed toward a particular figure or object. a relatively small group of people having religious beliefs or practices regarded by others as strange or sinister. "a network of Satan-worshiping cults"

2 Peter 2:1 (ESV)
2 But false prophets also arose among the people, just as there will be false teachers among you, who will secretly bring in destructive heresies, even denying the Master who bought them, bringing upon themselves swift destruction.

A GODLY PASTOR,

LIKE THE APOSTLE PAUL, WILL DEVOTE HIS LIFE TO SERVING JESUS CHRIST, AND FOLLOWING THE GREAT COMMISSION AND TEACHING GOD'S TRUTH TO ALL THOSE WHO WOULD LISTEN !

Matthew 28:19-20 (KJV)
[19] Go ye therefore, and teach all nations, baptizing them in the name of the Father, and of the Son, and of the Holy Ghost:
[20] Teaching them to observe all things whatsoever I have commanded you: and, lo, I am with you always, even unto the end of the world. Amen.

GODLY PASTORS WILL GIVE OF THEMSELVES TO THEIR CONGREGATIONS, AS THEY EXPECT THEIR CONGREGATIONS TO GIVE UNTO THEM ! A RARITY IN MOST OF TODAYS CHURCHES ! SELFISH, GREEDY, FALSE TEACHERS AND PREACHERS ARE ONLY INTERESTED IN THEMSELVES !

James 3:16 (NIV)
16 For where you have envy and selfish ambition, there you find disorder and every evil practice. Ephesians 4:19 (NIV)
19 Having lost all sensitivity, they have given themselves over to sensuality so as to indulge in every kind of impurity, and they are full of greed.

IF YOUR PASTOR WEARS SUITS AND SHOES THAT SHINE, TIES THAT DAZZLE, AND JEWELRY THAT GLITTERS, YOU MIGHT CONSIDER PAYING CLOSE ATTENTION TO THE SCRIPTURE HE USES IN HIS SERMONS!

Proverbs 11:28 King James Version (KJV)
[28] *He that trusteth in his riches shall fall; but the righteous shall flourish as a branch.*

Proverbs 22:16 King James Version (KJV)
[16] *He that oppresseth the poor to increase his riches, and he that giveth to the rich, shall surely come to want.*

Proverbs 8:10 King James Version (KJV)
[10] *Receive my instruction, and not silver; and knowledge rather than choice gold.*

IF YOUR PASTOR LIVES IN A MANSION ON A HILL HIGH ABOVE YOU, AND DRIVES A SHINY NEW LUXURY CAR, PAID FOR WITH YOUR HARD EARNED TITHES, HE'S PROBABLY A FALSE PREACHER !

Titus 1:16 (NIV)
16 They claim to know God, but by their actions they deny him. They are detestable, disobedient and unfit for doing anything good. Amos 3:15 (NIV)
15 I will tear down the winter house along with the summer house; the houses adorned with ivory will be destroyed and the mansions will be demolished, declares the LORD. Amos 5:11 (NIV)
You levy a straw tax on the poor and impose a tax on their grain. Therefore, though you have built stone mansions, you will not live in them; though you have planted lush vineyards, you will not drink their wine.

GODLY PASTORS, UNLIKE FALSE PREACHERS, WILL TEND THEIR FLOCK'S EVERYDAY NEEDS, EVERYDAY! THEY WILL NOT ABANDON THE FLOCK AFTER SUNDAYS SERMON! AS MANY DO TODAY! A TRUE FOLLOWER OF CHRIST WILL BE A DOER OF HIS GOSPEL AND FEED HIS SHEEP!

John 10:11 (NIV)
"I am the good shepherd. The good shepherd lays down his life for the sheep.

GODLY PASTORS
WILL NEVER STEAL THE LAST DOLLAR FROM THE IMPOVERISHED OR SENIORS IN THEIR FLOCK OF BELIEVERS, YET FALSE TEACHERS AND PREACHERS WON'T HESITATE TO PILFER FROM THEIR OWN CONGREGATION !

Romans 2:21 (NIV)

[21] you, then, who teach others, do you not teach yourself? You who preach against stealing, do you steal?

IF YOUR PASTOR LIVES ON A HORSE RANCH FAR AWAY FROM THE CITY AND ITS SINFUL INHABITANTS, AND DRIVES A FERRARI TO AND FROM CHURCH, HE MIGHT BE A FALSE PREACHER AND A REPROBATE!

Titus 1:16 King James Version (KJV)
[16] **They profess that they know God; but in works they deny him, being abominable, and disobedient, and unto every good work reprobate.**

2 Timothy 3:8 King James Version (KJV)
[8] **Now as Jannes and Jambres withstood Moses, so do these also resist the truth: men of corrupt minds, reprobate concerning the faith.**

FALSE TEACHERS AND PREACHERS ARE FILLED WITH BIBLICAL KNOWLEDGE ! WHICH DOES NOT SAVE ANYONE! THE DEVIL IS FILLED WITH IT! ALL FALSE PREACHERS ARE FILLED WITH IT ! WE NEED TO BE FILLED WITH THE HOLY SPIRIT AND THE GOSPEL TRUTH OF JESUS CHRIST !

Acts 4:31 (NIV)
[31] After they prayed, the place where they were meeting was shaken. And they were all filled with the Holy Spirit and spoke the word of God boldly.

CHURCHES THAT ARE LED

BY FALSE PREACHERS ARE DOING MORE DAMAGE TO THE CONGRATION THAN GOOD ! TEACHING YOU LIES AND A FALSE GOSPEL WILL LEAD YOU TO HELL, NOT HEAVEN ! ANY FALSE DOCTRINE IS OF THE DEVIL !

Proverbs 1:32 (NIV)
[32] For the waywardness of the simple will kill them, and the complacency of fools will destroy them;

Proverbs 14:11 (NIV)
11 The house of the wicked will be destroyed, but the tent of the upright will flourish.

FALSE TEACHERS AND PREACHERS

TWIST OLD TESTAMENT LAW TO SEDUCE YOU INTO ITS SPELL AND WEB OF LIES ! WE HAVE BEEN SET FREE FROM THE LAW BY THE "GRACE" OF GOD, AND THE SHED BLOOD OF HIS SON, JESUS CHRIST !

Romans 6:14 (KJV)
14 For sin shall not have dominion over you:
for ye are not under the law, but under grace.
2 Corinthians 12:9 (KJV)
And he said unto me, My grace is sufficient for thee:
for my strength is made perfect in weakness. Most
gladly therefore will I rather glory in my infirmities,
that the power of Christ may rest upon me.

FALSE TEACHERS AND PREACHERS PRODUCE ROTTEN FRUIT WITH THEIR FALSE TEACHING AND DOCTRINE ! THERE WILL BE NO ROTTEN FRUIT ALLOWED IN HEAVEN ! GOOD FRUIT CANNOT GROW IN THE DARKNESS OF FALSE DOCTRINE !

Matthew 7:16 (KJV)
[16] Ye shall know them by their fruits. Do men gather grapes of thorns, or figs of thistles?
Colossians 1:10 (KJV)
10 That ye might walk worthy of the Lord unto all pleasing, being fruitful in every good work, and increasing in the knowledge of God;

THE LIGHT OF JESUS CHRIST

THAT WE EXPECT TO FIND IN OUR CHURCHES TODAY, ISN'T THERE IF A FALSE PREACHER IS COVERING IT WITH THE DARKNESS OF FALSE DOCTRINE AND THE EVIL OF DECEPTION !

John 8:12 (KJV)

[12] *Then spake Jesus again unto them, saying, I am the light of the world: he that followeth me shall not walk in darkness, but shall have the light of life.*

John 3:19 (KJV)

19 And this is the condemnation, that light is come into the world, and men loved darkness rather than light, because their deeds were evil.

FALSE DOCTRINE

IS SCRIPTURE TWISTED OUT OF CONTEXT BY BLIND GUIDES, FALSE TEACHERS, AND PREACHERS TO DECEIVE AND BLIND GOD'S CHILDREN FROM HIS TRUTH AND LEAD THEM ASTRAY ! WE MUST BE VIGILANT AND STUDY THE SCRIPTURE DAILY TO CONFIRM OUR PASTORS SERMONS !

Acts 17: (NIV)

Now the Berean Jews were of more noble character than those in Thessalonica, for they received the message with great eagerness and examined the Scriptures every day to see if what Paul said was true.

MANY FALSE TEACHERS AND PREACHERS

WANT YOU TO BELIEVE THERE ARE SHORTCUTS YOU CAN TAKE ALONG THE NARROW PATH TO ETERNAL LIFE! THERE ARE NOT! WHEN WE FALL OFF, WE MUST GET RIGHT BACK ON!

Matthew 7:14 (NIV)
14 But small is the gate and narrow the road that leads to life, and only a few find it.
Matthew 15:14 (KJV)
14 Let them alone: they be blind leaders of the blind. And if the blind lead the blind, both shall fall into the ditch.

TRAVELING THE NARROW ROAD

TO ETERNAL LIFE CAN BE EXTREMELY DANGEROUS WITH SO MANY RAVENOUS WOLVES, BLIND GUIDES, PREACHERS, AND TEACHERS SEEKING TO DEVOUR YOU THROUGHOUT YOUR JOURNEY WITH CHRIST !

Matthew 7:13-14 (NIV)
The Narrow and Wide Gates
13 *"Enter through the narrow gate. For wide is the gate and broad is the road that leads to destruction, and many enter through it. 14 But small is the gate and narrow the road that leads to life, and only a few find it.*

FALSE TEACHINGS AND DOCTRINE

CREATE A DARKNESS IN OUR CHURCHES THAT SUNLIGHT CAN'T BREAK THROUGH ! GOOD FRUIT DOESN'T GROW IN THE DARKNESS, ONLY ROTTEN FRUIT !

Matthew 7:16 (KJV)
16 Ye shall know them by their fruits. Do men gather grapes of thorns, or figs of thistles?
Matthew 7:17 (KJV)
17 Even so every good tree bringeth forth good fruit; but a corrupt tree bringeth forth evil fruit.

LET THERE BE LIGHT

IN YOUR CHURCH ! ONLY THE LIGHT AND TRUTH OF GODS SON, JESUS CHRIST HAS THE POWER TO PRODUCE GOOD FRUIT AND ILLUMINATE THE EVIL AND BAD FRUIT THAT FALSE PREACHERS PRODUCE !

John 8:12 (KJV)

Then spoke Jesus again unto them, saying, I am the light of the world: he that followeth me shall not walk in darkness, but shall have the light of life.

Matthew 3:8 (KJV)

8 Bring forth therefore fruits meet for repentance:

MANY FALSE TEACHERS AND PREACHERS

PREY ON, AND TAKE ADVANTAGE OF SENIORS AND THE HANDICAPPED WHO ARE DISADVANTAGED AND VULNERABLE TO THE EVIL CUNNINGNESS OF THESE CULPRITS BEHIND THE PULPITS !

Matthew 10:16 (KJV)
Behold, I send you forth as sheep in the midst of wolves: be ye therefore wise as serpents, and harmless as doves. Romans 2:21 (NIV)
you, then, who teach others, do you not teach yourself? You who preach against stealing, do you steal?

MANY FALSE TEACHERS AND PREACHERS PREY ON, AND TAKE ADVANTAGE OF WIDOWS, DIVORCEES, AND SINGLE WOMAN ! AS DISGUSTING AS IT MAY SEEM, IT HAPPENS ALL DAY LONG IN MANY DARK CHURCHES BY PERVERTED EVIL FALSE PREACHERS !

Mark 12:40 (NIV)
[40] They devour widows' houses and for a show make lengthy prayers. These men will be punished most severely."

IF FALSE TEACHERS AND PREACHERS

WHO ARE SCHOOLED IN DECEPTION BY SATAN, CAN USE AND TWIST SCRIPTURE TO DECIEVE THE MOST EDUCATED THEOLOGIAN, THEY CAN MOST ASSUREDLY DECEIVE THE LOST SHEEP WHO ARE SEEKING SHELTER FROM THE STORMS !

Acts 17:11 (KJV)
[11] These were more noble than those in Thessalonica, in that they received the word with all readiness of mind, and searched the scriptures daily, whether those things were so.

MANY FALSE TEACHERS AND PREACHERS

KEEP DRUNKARDS DRUNK, AND ADDICTS ADDICTED, BY PROMOTING AND ENDORSING SECULAR ADDICTION RECOVERY PROGRAMS THAT USE WORLDLY PHILOSOPHY TO CURE A DISEASE THAT DOESN'T EXIST ! DRUNKENNESS IS A SIN, NOT A DISEASE !

Colossians 2:8 (NIV)
See to it that no one takes you captive through hollow and deceptive philosophy, which depends on human tradition and the elemental spiritual forces.

THERE SHOULD BE NO VISIBLE EVIDENCE

OF THE WORLD IN YOUR CHURCH OR YOUR PASTORS SERMONS! MOST OF TODAYS CHURCHES MIMICK THE WORLD, AS THEY ABANDON THE GOSPEL OF JESUS CHRIST AND THE CHRISTIANS WHO SEEK TO LIVE AND BE SAVED BY IT !

John 18:36 (KJV)

36 Jesus answered, My kingdom is not of this world: John 10:12 (NIV) The hired hand is not the shepherd and does not own the sheep. So when he sees the wolf coming, he abandons the sheep and runs away. Then the wolf attacks the flock and scatters it.

FALSE TEACHERS AND PREACHERS ARE NOT SAVED, BORN AGAIN CHRISTIANS ! SAVED, BORN AGAIN CHRISTIANS DO NOT DECIEVE OTHERS WITH BLASPHEMOUS DOCTRINE AND HERESY ! THEIR DIRTY DEEDS WILL LEAD THEM TO HELL, NOT HEAVEN !

Acts 26:20 (NIV)
[20] First to those in Damascus, then to those in Jerusalem and in all Judea, and then to the Gentiles, I preached that they should repent and turn to God and demonstrate their repentance by their deeds.

THE LOST SHEEP WILL FOLLOW THEIR BLIND GUIDES !

IF THEIR FALSE PREACHER ISN'T FOLLOWING AND SERVING CHRIST, THEY NEED TO FIND A CHURCH LED BY A GODLY PASTOR! A CHALLENGING TASK IN TODAYS DARK WORLD OF CHURCHES!

Matthew 15:14 (NIV)
14 Leave them; they are blind guides.
If the blind lead the blind, both will fall into a pit."

LOST SHEEP WILL FOLLOW THEIR BLIND GUIDES

OVER A CLIFF IF THEY AREN'T VIGILANT AND SEARCH AND STUDY THE SCRIPTURE DAILY TO SEE IF WHAT THEIR PASTORS SAY IS FROM THE GOSPEL OF JESUS CHRIST !

Acts 17:11 (NIV)

[11] Now the Berean Jews were of more noble character than those in Thessalonica, for they received the message with great eagerness and examined the Scriptures every day to see if what Paul said was true.

MILLIONS OF BORN AGAIN CHRISTIANS ARE TURNING AWAY FROM THEIR CHURCHES IN DESPAIR AND CONFUSION AS THEY HELPLESSLY WATCH THEIR BROTHERS AND SISTERS IN CHRIST BEING DECEIVED AND LED ASTRAY BY THEIR FALSE PREACHERS !

Galatians 4:9 (NIV)
[9] But now that you know God—or rather are known by God—how is it that you are turning back to those weak and miserable forces ? Do you wish to be enslaved by them all over again?

FALSE TEACHERS AND PREACHERS ARE FILLED WITH THEMSELVES RATHER THAN THE HOLY SPIRIT ! THEY ARE FILLED WITH PRIDE AND EGO ALONG WITH ARROGANCE AND SELF- RIGHTEOUSNESS, SPENDING MOST OF THEIR TIME IN FRONT OF A MIRROR PRACTICING THEIR DECEPTION!

Ephesians 4:23-25 (NIV)
[23] to be made new in the attitude of your minds; [24] and to put on the new self, created to be like God in true righteousness and holiness. [25] Therefore each of you must put off falsehood and speak truthfully to your neighbor, for we are all members of one body.

MILLIONS OF LOST SOULS,

SICK AND HANDI-CAPPED, WIDOWS, SENIORS, AND OTHER VULNERABLE SINNERS ATTEND CHURCHES TODAY SEEKING SHELTER FROM THE STORMS OF LIFE IN THIS DARK EVIL WORLD, ONLY TO FIND THE SAME DARKNESS COMING FROM BEHIND THE PULPIT !

John 1:5 (NIV)

5 The light shines in the darkness, and the darkness has not overcome it. Matthew 4:16 (NIV) the people living in darkness have seen a great light; on those living in the land of the shadow of death a light has dawned."

BEWARE !
FALSE DOCTRINE
LEADS TO DEATH, NOT ETERNAL LIFE WITH JESUS CHRIST ! OUR CHURCHES TODAY ARE FILLED WITH FALSE DOCTRINE CREATED THROUGH THE DECEPTION OF FALSE TEACHERS AND PREACHERS !

1 Timothy 4:1-2-16 (NIV)
4 The Spirit clearly says that in later times some will abandon the faith and follow deceiving spirits and things taught by demons. ² Such teachings come through hypocritical liars, whose consciences have been seared as with a hot iron. ¹⁶ Watch your life and doctrine closely. Persevere in them, because if you do, you will save both yourself and your hearers.

BEWARE !

DON'T BE DECEIVED !

FALSE TEACHERS AND PREACHERS CANNOT SAVE YOU, HEAL YOU, FREE YOU, OR ANSWER ANY OF YOUR PRAYERS, NO MATTER HOW MUCH MONEY YOU TITHE TO THEM ! INSPITE OF WHAT MANY OF THEM ARE TELLING YOU !

2 Peter 3:17 (KJV)
[17] Ye therefore, beloved, seeing ye know these things before, beware lest ye also, being led away with the error of the wicked, fall from your own stedfastness.

IT IS CRUCIAL

THAT TODAYS CHRISTIANS PROTECT THEMSELVES FROM THE FALSE TEACHERS AND PREACHERS THAT TRY TO DECEIVE THEM AND LEAD THEM AWAY FROM THE GOSPEL OF JESUS CHRIST, BY WEARING THE FULL ARMOR OF GOD !

Read Ephesians 6:10-18 (NIV)
[10] Finally, be strong in the Lord and in his mighty power. [11] Put on the full armor of God, so that you can take your stand against the devil's schemes. [12] For our struggle is not against flesh and blood, but against the rulers, against the authorities, against the powers of this dark world and against the spiritual forces of evil in the heavenly realms. [13] Therefore put on the full armor of God, so that when the day of evil comes, you may be able to stand your ground, and after you have done everything, to stand.

THERE IS A DARKNESS

THAT HAS ENGULFED OUR CHURCHES UNLIKE ANY WE'VE EVER SEEN BEFORE! OUR HOPE IS IN THE FACT THAT WE HAVE BEEN WARNED OF THESE DARK, EVIL, DAYS IN BIBLICAL PROPHECY THROUGHOUT GODS WORD, AND NOW THEY ARE HERE AMONG US TODAY !

John 8:12 (NIV)
[12] When Jesus spoke again to the people, he said, "I am the light of the world. Whoever follows me will never walk in darkness, but will have the light of life."

IF YOUR PASTOR DOESN'T TEACH THE IMPORTANCE OF REPENTANCE, THEN YOUR SALVATION MAY BE AT RISK AND YOU NEED TO WARN THE CONGREGATION TO FLEE THE WOLF LEADING YOUR CHURCH ! MANY FALSE PREACHERS ARE AVOIDING THE SUBJECT TO ATTRACT A BIGGER AUDIENCE !

Acts 26:20 (NIV)

[20] First to those in Damascus, then to those in Jerusalem and in all Judea, and then to the Gentiles, I preached that they should repent and turn to God and demonstrate their repentance by their deeds.

FALSE PREACHING HAS LED MUCH OF THE UN-SAVED WORLD INTO BELIEVING THEY CAN BE SAVED BY PRAYING A SIMPLE PRAYER, BEING BAPTIZED, AND TITHING, OR "GIFTING" A SUM OF MONEY TO PAY FOR THEIR SALVATION ! YOUR SALVATION WAS BOUGHT AND PAID FOR ON THE CROSS !

Acts 20:28 (NIV)
28 Keep watch over yourselves and all the flock of which the Holy Spirit has made you overseers. Be shepherds of the church of God, which he bought with his own blood.

YOU ARE BETTER OFF

BEING ALONE IN THIS WORLD WITH JESUS AT YOUR SIDE, KNOWING YOU'RE GOING TO HEAVEN, THEN BEING SURROUNDED BY LOST SOULS BEING DECEIVED AND MISLED BY FALSE PREACHERS LEADING YOU AND THE CONGREGATION TO HELL !

Isaiah 5:20 (NIV)
[20] Woe to those who call evil good and good evil, who put darkness for light and light for darkness, who put bitter for sweet and sweet for bitter.

BEING DECEIVED IS EASY

WHEN YOUR FALSE PREACHER KNOWS YOU'RE NOT READING YOUR BIBLE ! YOUR SALVATION IS AT STAKE AND IN YOUR HANDS ! IT IS UP TO YOU TO ENSURE YOU ARE BEING TAUGHT THE GOSPEL TRUTH OF JESUS CHRIST !

Acts 17:11 (NIV)
[11] Now the Berean Jews were of more noble character than those in Thessalonica, for they received the message with great eagerness and examined the Scriptures every day to see if what Paul said was true.

FALSE PREACHERS AND TEACHERS

WHO DON'T SUPPORT AND PROMOTE MISSIONARIES ARE IGNORING THE GOSPEL MESSAGE OF CHRISTS GREAT COMMISSION IN

Matthew 28: 16-20
The Great Commission

16 Then the eleven disciples went to Galilee, to the mountain where Jesus had told them to go. 17 When they saw him, they worshiped him; but some doubted. 18 Then Jesus came to them and said, "All authority in heaven and on earth has been given to me. 19 Therefore go and make disciples of all nations, baptizing them in the name of the Father and of the Son and of the Holy Spirit, 20 and teaching them to obey everything I have commanded you. And surely I am with you always, to the very end of the age."

MUCH OF THE EVIL WE FIND BEHIND THE MASKS THAT FALSE TEACHERS AND PREACHERS WEAR IS DONE BEHIND CLOSED DOORS IN COUNSELING SESSIONS IN PASTOR'S OFFICES ! MILLIONS OF INNOCENT LOST SHEEP ARE VICTIMIZED AND ROBBED EVERY DAY THROUGH DECEIT AND GREED !

Proverbs 12:20 (NIV)
[20] Deceit is in the hearts of those who plot evil,
but those who promote peace have joy.
Proverbs 26:24 (NIV)
24 Enemies disguise themselves with their lips,
but in their hearts they harbor deceit.

BEWARE !

PRIVATE COUNSELING IS THE REAL BREAD-MAKER FOR THE CON-ARTISTS WHO ARE FALSE TEACHERS AND PREACHERS WHO USE THEIR POSITION AND POWER TO SWINDLE HOMES AND FORTUNES FROM SENIORS AND OTHER VULNERABLE MEMBERS OF THERE CHURCHES !

Proverbs 26:24 (NIV)
24 Enemies disguise themselves with their lips,
but in their hearts they harbor deceit.

MILLIONS OF CHRISTIANS

SEEK GODLY COUNSELING EVERYDAY AND TRUST THEIR PASTORS FOR THE BEST ADVICE "MONEY CAN BUY"! A PART OF THE "PROSPERITY GOSPEL" THAT MAKES FALSE PREACHERS RICH BY CONVINCING MEMBERS TO "DIG DEEPER" TO PAY FOR ANSWERED PRAYERS!

Proverbs 12:20 (NIV)
[20] Deceit is in the hearts of those who plot evil, but those who promote peace have joy.

FALSE TEACHERS AND PREACHERS KEEP THEIR FLOCK IN THE DARK BY REJECTING AND HIDING THE GOSPEL TRUTH AND THE SHED BLOOD OF JESUS CHRIST ON THE CROSS, AND FOCUSING ON OLD TESTAMENT LEGALISM ! LET THE LIGHT OF JESUS SHINE ON YOUR LIFE !

John 8:12 (KJV)
12 Then spake Jesus again unto them, saying, I am the light of the world: he that followeth me shall not walk in darkness, but shall have the light of life.

THE PROSPERITY GOSPEL

IS AS OLD AS FALSE PROPHETS! AS GREED IS THE ROOT TO ALL EVIL! MILLIONS OF LOST SHEEP HAVE BEEN VICTIMIZED BY FALSE TEACHERS AND PREACHERS FOR CENTURIES, AND AS A RESULT, MANY HAVE TURNED FROM THEIR FAITH !

1 Timothy 4:1 (NLT)
4 Now the Holy Spirit tells us clearly that in the last times some will turn away from the true faith; they will follow deceptive spirits and teachings that come from demons.

BEWARE OF ...
SWEET TALKING
FALSE TEACHERS
AND PREACHERS

WHO HAVE THEIR CONGREGATIONS DECEIVED INTO BELIEVING THEY ARE ANGELS FROM HEAVEN SENT BY GOD TO RESCUE YOU, SAVE YOU, HEAL YOU, AND BLESS YOU WITH WEALTH !

2 Corinthians 11:14 (NIV)
[14] And no wonder, for Satan himself masquerades as an angel of light.

SATAN'S FALSE TEACHERS AND PREACHERS

PEDDLE THEIR PERVERTED DOCTRINE MASQUERADING AS ANGELS OF LIGHT ! DECEIVING NOT JUST THE LOST SHEEP IN THE WORLD, BUT EVEN THE MOST WELL READ, VERSED, AND EDUCATED !

2 Corinthians 11:14 (NIV)
And no wonder, for Satan himself masquerades as an angel of light. Matthew 7:15-16 (ESV)
"Beware of false prophets, who come to you in sheep's clothing but inwardly are ravenous wolves. 16 You will recognize them by their fruits. Are grapes gathered from thornbushes, or figs from thistles?

PROSPERITY GOSPEL VS. POVERTY GOSPEL !

TWO OPPOSING FALSE GOSPELS CREATED BY FALSE PREACHERS TO CONDEMN THEIR CONGREGATIONS INTO GUILT THAT CAN ONLY BE RESOLVED THROUGH TITHING GENEROUSLY TO PLEASE GOD

Proverbs 1:32 (KJV)
[32] For the turning away of the simple shall slay them, and the prosperity of fools shall destroy them.
Romans 2:21 (ESV)
you then who teach others, do you not teach yourself? While you preach against stealing, do you steal?

GODLY PASTORS
ARE ONLY CONCERNED ABOUT SERVING THE LOST SHEEP AND PLEASING GOD BY FOLLOWING THE GOSPEL TRUTH OF JESUS CHRIST! WHILE FALSE TEACHERS AND PREACHERS ARE ONLY CONCERNED ABOUT PLEASING AND FEEDING THEMSELVES!

Jeremiah 3:15 (KJV) And I will give you pastors according to mine heart, which shall feed you with knowledge and understanding. Matthew 4:10 (NIV)[10] Jesus said to him, "Away from me, Satan! For it is written: 'Worship the Lord your God, and serve him only." Isaiah 57:17 (NIV) I was enraged by their sinful greed; I punished them, and hid my face in anger, yet they kept on in their willful ways.

THE PROSPERITY GOSPEL

IS FOUND IN MOST CHURCHES TODAY THROUGH THE MISUSE OF SCRIPTURE TO HEAP GUILT ON THE SHEEP AND CONVINCE THEM THAT GOD HATES THOSE WHO DON'T GIVE THEIR LAST DOLLAR IN THE TITHE TO FEED THE FAT PREACHER WHILE THE GIVER STARVES!

1 Timothy 6:9 (ESV)
[9] But those who desire to be rich fall into temptation, into a snare, into many senseless and harmful desires that plunge people into ruin and destruction.

THE PROSPERITY GOSPEL

FOCUSES ON "GIVING" TO THE FALSE TEACHERS AND PREACHERS BY "TAKING" FROM THE POOR AND LESS FORTUNATE, RATHER THAN "SERVING" THE LORD AND HIS PEOPLE ! THE FALSE DOCTRINE OF PROSPERITY HAS DRIVEN MILLIONS FROM THE CHURCH !

1 Timothy 6:9 (ESV) But those who desire to be rich fall into temptation, into a snare, into many senseless and harmful desires that plunge people into ruin and destruction.
Proverbs 28:6 (ESV)
[6] Better is a poor man who walks in his integrity than a rich man who is crooked in his ways.

THE PROSPERITY GOSPEL

OFTEN CONSISTS OF "PAYING" OR (TITHING MORE) FOR ANSWERED PRAYERS FOR HEALING, HEALTH, WEALTH, AND EVEN SALVATION ! FALSE TEACHERS AND PREACHERS ARE A BREED OF VIPERS ONLY LOVED BY SATAN !

Matthew 23:33 (KJV)
[33] Ye serpents, ye generation of vipers, how can ye escape the damnation of hell?
Matthew 12:34 (ESV) You brood of vipers! How can you speak good, when you are evil? For out of the abundance of the heart the mouth speaks.

KEEPING THE LAW, OR LEGALISM

IS ANOTHER FALSE DOCTRINE FALSE TEACHERS AND PREACHERS USE TO KEEP THEIR FLOCK IN THE DARK, AND THEIR BANK ACCOUNTS FLOURISHING ! THE LAW WAS ABOLISHED ON THE CROSS WITH THE SACRIFICE OF JESUS CHRIST

Galatians 3:24 (ESV)
24 So then, the law was our guardian until Christ came, in order that we might be justified by faith.

John 1:17 King James Version (KJV)
17 For the law was given by Moses, but grace and truth came by Jesus Christ.

FROM THE LIPS OF THE SERPENT,

AKA, THE FALSE PREACHER IN YOUR FRIENDLY NEIGHBORHOOD CHURCH, YOU MAY HEAR SOME OF THE FOLLOWING WORDS IN THE SAME SENTENCE; "YOU WERE SAVED BY GRACE, AS LONG AS YOU TITHE!" OR; "YOUR SIN IS FORGIVEN, IF YOU TITHE", AND MANY MORE SIMILAR LIES !

Genesis 3:1 (NIV) Now the serpent was more crafty than any of the wild animals the LORD God had made. He said to the woman, "Did God really say, 'You must not eat from any tree in the garden'?"

APOSTACY IS THE FRUIT OF FALSE DOCTRINE !

IT IS CREATED BY FALSE TEACHERS AND PREACHERS WHO DON'T PREACH THE GOSPEL TRUTH OF JESUS CHRIST, BECAUSE THEY DON'T KNOW THE AUTHOR ! CAUSING MANY CHRISTIANS TO FALL AWAY FROM CHRIST AND ABANDON THEIR FAITH !

1 Timothy 4:1 (ESV)
Now the Spirit expressly says that in later times some will depart from the faith by devoting themselves to deceitful spirits and teachings of demons,

FALSE DOCTRINE

IS AS RAMPANT IN THE CHURCH TODAY AS THE FALSE TEACHERS AND PREACHERS WHO CREATE IT ! FOR ALMOST EVERY TOPIC AND SUBJECT WE FIND IN GODS WORD TODAY, THERE IS A FALSE PREACHER CHANGING ITS AUTHENTICITY BY USING SCRIPTURE OUT OF CONTEXT, OR ELIMINATING IT COMPLETELY !

Hebrews 13:9 (NIV)
9 Do not be carried away by all kinds of strange teachings. It is good for our hearts to be strengthened by grace, not by eating ceremonial foods, which is of no benefit to those who do so.

GODS "TRUTH" IS THE ONLY "PROOF"

WE NEED TO PROVE THAT MOST OF OUR CHURCHES ARE NOW LED BY SATAN MASQUERADING AS FALSE TEACHERS AND PREACHERS LEADING THEIR FLOCKS TO HELL ! THE PROOF IS IN THE SCRIPTURE FROM BEGINNING TO END !

Acts 17:31 (NIV)
31 For he has set a day when he will judge the world with justice by the man he has appointed. He has given proof of this to everyone by raising him from the dead."

SPIRITUAL DISCERNMENT

IS NOT A TOPIC OR SUBJECT FALSE TEACHERS AND PREACHERS WANT THEIR CONGREGATION TO STUDY ABOUT. OR IT WILL REVEAL THE MANY MASKS OF EVIL AND DECEPTION THEY ARE WEARING ! WHILE IT OPENS OUR EYES TO GODS TRUTH !

Romans 12:2 (ESV)
²Do not be conformed to this world, but be transformed by the renewal of your mind, that by testing you may discern what is the will of God, what is good and acceptable and perfect.

THE CHURCH

IS DEAD! THE FEW THAT ARE STILL BREATHING, ARE SUFFOCATING FROM POLLUTION CREATED BY FALSE TEACHERS AND PREACHERS! THE REMNANT WILL SURVIVE ONLY BY FOLLOWING THE GOSPEL TRUTH OF JESUS CHRIST WITHOUT COMPROMISE!

1 Timothy 4:1-2 (ESV)
Now the Spirit expressly says that in later times some will depart from the faith by devoting themselves to deceitful spirits and teachings of demons, [2] through the insincerity of liars whose consciences are seared, 2 Timothy 4:3 For the time is coming when people will not endure sound[a] teaching, but having itching ears they will accumulate for themselves teachers to suit their own passions,

CONCLUSION ...
MANY, PERHAPS MILLIONS OF BORN-AGAIN, GOD-FEARING CHRISTIANS HAVE LEFT THEIR CHURCHES AND PERHAPS ABANDONED THEIR FAITH BECAUSE OF BAD EXPERIENCES DUE TO FALSE DOCTRINE CREATED BY SATAN THROUGH THE DARK, EVIL MOUTHS AND MINDS OF FALSE PREACHERS, TEACHERS, AND BLIND GUIDES WHO THEMSELVES HAVE BEEN DECEIVED BY SATAN THROUGH THEIR OWN IGNORANCE! JUST LIKE DRUNKARDS, THEY ARE IN DENIAL OF THEIR SIN, AND SEE NO HARM IN THEIR EVIL BEHAVIOR! THEY ARE CLUELESS TO THE DEVASTATION AND ETERNAL DEATH THEY CAUSE MILLIONS OF INNOCENT LOST SOULS WHO ARE SEEKING SHELTER FROM THE MANY STORMS OF LIFE ! I HOPE THIS BOOK HAS EXPOSED MANY OF THE MASKS THESE ANGELS OF SATAN WEAR TO DECEIVE THE FLOCK AND LEAD THEM AWAY FROM GODS TRUTH !

These Messages Have Been Written by a Mere Common Pilgrim and Brother in Christ, to be Read And Hopefully Comprehended by Those Traveling The Same Narrow Path as I.

A Brother in Christ,

Don Johnson

May The Spirit of God Rest On You As You Grow And Mature in The Gospel Truth of Our Lord And Savior, Jesus Christ! Thank You in Advance for Sharing These Words of Truth With Others!

It Is My Prayer That Anyone Who May Have Been Led Astray From

Their Faith in Their Lord
And Savior, Jesus Christ,
Through The False Teachings
Of A False Preacher, Will
Find Their Way Back
Through The Messages,
Words, And Scripture Found
In This Book. It Was
Written To Expose The
Heresy, Blasphemy, And
False Doctrine We Find In

Many Of Our Churches Today Led By False Teachers And Preachers To Deceive Gods People And Lead Them Away From His Truth And Salvation !

Amen !

Luke 21:8 (KJV)
[8] And he said, Take heed that ye be not deceived: for many shall come in my name, saying, I am Christ; and the time draweth near: go ye not therefore after them.

NOTES

NOTES

NOTES

Made in the USA
Middletown, DE
08 July 2021